Money:

Athlete Career Killer

100 Money Tips for Athletes

David L. Brown

PLAY HARD.™ DO GOOD.™
CharacterAthletic.com™

ISBN-10 = 0982664184
ISBN-13 = 978-0-9826641-8-6

First Edition – *Athlete Career Killer* ™ series of books
Published by Parkway Press, Ltd.™ Niles, Ohio
www.parkwaypress.com
Printed in the United States of America

Media Interview Contact:
David L. Brown,
Founder and President
Character Athletic, Ltd.
P.O. Box 5061
Niles, Ohio 44446-7061
United States
330-505-8113
E-mail: dlbrown88@yahoo.com

Play Hard. Do Good.™
www.CharacterAthletic.com
www.AthleteCareerKiller.com

Athletes will enjoy reading, and benefit from the valuable and potentially life saving information in the author's Athlete Career Killer™ series.

Clubbing: Athlete Career Killer™

Drunk Driving: Athlete Career Killer™

Guns: Athlete Career Killer™

Drugs: Athlete Career Killer™

Domestic Violence: Athlete Career Killer™

Infidelity: Athlete Career Killer™

Home Invasion: Athlete Career Killer™

Gambling: Athlete Career Killer™

Money: Athlete Career Killer ™

College Academics: Athlete Career Killer™

POPS™: Athlete Career Savior™

3RD Down and God: #1 Spiritual Guide for Athletes™

The author believes the entire Athlete Career Killer™ book series should be placed in the hands of all professional athletes. All student-athletes, and all incoming freshman student-athletes who commit to continue their athletic and academic careers in a college or university football and basketball program, should also be handed the complete Athlete Career Killer™ book series as part of an orientation program upon signing. The same with every draft class in the NFL, NBA, NHL, and Major League Baseball.

Consider this book series an investment — an investment in your athletes, your teams, your schools, your organizations, your leagues, and your communities.

Dedication

Thank you, *Almighty God*!

To my late father, Jim, whom we lovingly called "Pops." Thank you for giving me the gift of my last name — *Brown*. There is a very important word within my last name that you instilled in me and inspired in me — *Own*! You taught me that if you don't "own" your own life and make it everything you want it to be — somebody else will!

To Brandon and Alýssa. Thank you for being great kids since the day you were born! You are both smart, witty, respectful, and you listen when Dad imparts wisdom. You each love to laugh, and you love life. Always stay true to that in your heart — don't ever let anyone change that in you!

Acknowledgments

Mom, thank you for bringing me into this world. I wouldn't be here without *you*! To Sharon, Jim, and Danae — much love always. Honoring my late sister, Buena. I miss you.

To editors Jim and Sue Long. You are nothing short of class in every way! Visit them at agoodedit.com. Tell them *David Brown* sent you!

"Athletes who often look invincible on the field and court are often financially vulnerable off it. Know that you CAN put your financial life back on track and recover from a major financial loss. For those athletes that have, I am proud of you — and you should be proud too."

David L. Brown

Contents

Introduction

Short Career Lifespan

You've worked hard to get to the professional level. You've earned that opportunity and the money that comes with it. Now you must work even harder to keep it!

The average length of an NFL career is about three and a half seasons. The average length for NBA athletes is about five seasons. Athletes leave the game because of injury, making poor decisions off the field, self-induced retirement, or being cut by the team. This also means that while athletes may make more money than most people, they are only making it for an average of three and a half years. To make sure they are successful in the future, athletes must invest their money well and make plans for their next career when they can no longer play football, basketball, baseball or hockey.

It's about financial responsibility and accountability.

That's what this book is all about. A practical, easy to read and understand financial guide for all athletes, especially professional athletes. This book, along with the other titles in my 12-book Athlete Career Killer™ series, will give you a substantial amount of "*takeaways*." In sports, a takeaway is when an athlete takes the ball away from the other team and runs with it!

So take away the many practical tips contained in this book — and run with them, to help you improve your long-term financial standing!

The truth is — if an athlete doesn't manage his money well during his playing career, he'll be left with dealing with the consequences of not having enough money after retirement from the game. The NBA Player's Association, for example, has continually offered a financial firm that gives athletes free second opinions on their finances. That's the easy part. Getting them to act is the big challenge!

Also, there's an issue with athletes having children out of wedlock. This is yet another expense, in addition to the cars, houses, expensive jewelry, lavish spending on entertainment, etc., that must be accounted for. Child support is an expense that doesn't go away for at least 18 years. A professional athlete five years removed from the game, with two to three (or more) monthly child support payments, can easily and quickly run out of money.

Consider this: The average length of your professional career is short, maybe 3-5 years, if you're lucky. In the United States, male life expectancy in 2010 is 75.6 years. So if you're a thirty-year-old professional athlete retiring this year, you still have another forty-five years of life to live!

Do you really need to buy another car, house, more expensive jewelry, or have another woman on the side?

Chapter 1

You're Wealthy — Now What?

There's a perfect storm of inexperience, ignorance, peer pressure, bad advice, and multimillion dollar contracts that make it difficult for a professional athlete to hold onto wealth long term. They need smart financial advice just like everyone else — perhaps more so. The sad truth is, most of the time they don't get it, or they simply ignore it.

There are many people in the financial industry who will gladly profit from the ignorance of an athlete's newfound wealth. And it's not just lousy advice that creates the problem. Athletes themselves are prone to making poor choices regarding their money, especially when they're young.

Some athletes, young and older, attempt to sustain and maintain a "*Rolls Royce*" lifestyle. If they choose the smart way to go and save their money now, they have a better chance of living comfortably for the rest of their lives after retirement.

Recession or no recession, some NFL, NBA, NHL, and Major League Baseball athletes have a penchant for losing most or all of their money, regardless of how much they make.

Here's one indulgence I guarantee professional athletes will enjoy when their playing days are long over — hindsight. It's the old *"I wish I would've, could've, should've"* syndrome.

Another issue I see in speaking with professional athletes is that contracts, financial agreements, investments, brokers, attorneys, accountants — the language of those industries sound foreign to them. In many cases, athletes lack the time and desire to understand and monitor their investments. Some lose any interest in educating themselves about the various financial products on the market today and the legally binding complexities of a business deal.

Here's one answer to that problem —*Ask questions!* Don't ever be afraid to question authority! If something doesn't sound right, feel right, or read right — ask questions, and don't stop asking until you feel comfortable with the answers. It's all about due diligence and the desire to *educate yourself.* Yes, due diligence and education are hard work, but it's hard work that will pay you a higher dividend in the future than that portfolio of stocks you own.

Did You Know? Athletes have a different set of financial challenges than, say, entertainers. Why? Because there is a far shorter "peak earnings period" in sports than in any other profession. Entertainers can perform and earn a good living well into their senior citizen years!

A professional athlete's money is supposed to outlive his career. Be the athlete who can say, *"Yeah, I get that,"* and strive to form a solid financial game plan around it. You must acquire some *financial savvy* about yourself.

Our current anemic economic condition also increases the anxiety in professional athletes, especially those closer to retirement or those who have recently retired. We've all heard the sad but true stories of former professional athletes selling their championship and Super Bowl rings, trophies, and other sports memorabilia as a disheartened and embarrassing last resort.

If you're a veteran professional athlete and you see a teammate, especially a young teammate, heading toward financial disaster, don't be afraid to speak up and speak out! Impart some of your wisdom, and talk to them about your own experiences. If you have to, insist they partake in a financial "intervention."

We can no longer sit back and watch our athletes become ignorant of their own financial affairs, ignorant of the people who handle their money, and continue to watch athletes' lives end in financial ruin.

According to the NFL Players Association, at least 78 players lost a total of more than $42 million between 1999 and 2002 because they trusted money to financial advisers with questionable backgrounds. I can only imagine what those figures were in 2009! Know that even when athletes trust financiers of high reputation, things can still go terribly wrong. No financial planner, adviser, consultant, broker, wealth or fund manager is perfect — they make mistakes, too, which can cripple your financial well-being for life.

You love playing sports with your teammates and other athletes in your league. It's a tremendous bonding experience — a true brethren. But please avoid stock tips, business investment tips, or hedge fund tips from teammates, other athletes, coaches, or former athletes. It's not that they're bad people; in most cases they're not. It's just that a person who manages money must have a certain "skill set" that is legal, licensed, and registered with the SEC (Securities and Exchange Commission), which is required by law of any investment advisory firm with at least $25 million in assets under management.

Giving or receiving stock market tips or financial advice to a teammate is the easiest and quickest way to lose a good friend! Most people don't understand, nor have the patience for the high-low reality known as the stock market. Stock market values increase, decrease, or remain relatively flat. Resist the temptation when someone asks for advice. Instead, give them the business card of your trusted, licensed financial planner and leave it at that.

Also, keep an eye out for the dreaded and financially disastrous *Ponzi scheme*! What's a Ponzi scheme? In short, it's a fraudulent investment operation that pays returns to investors from their own money, or money paid by subsequent investors rather than from any actual profit earned.

Be careful purchasing real estate as investment property. In today's economy, especially in real estate, anything you bought in the last two years is likely upside down, meaning its value has significantly depreciated and is currently not worth what you initially paid for it.

I GUARANTEE THIS — when you become a professional athlete, new people you've never met will beat a path to your door. People, including family members and friends you haven't seen or heard from in years, will want you to loan them money, help them find a job, invest in a business deal, or try to get you to hire them to work for you in some capacity. Countless women will want to date you, marry you and have your children, and a host of other things. Be bold, have courage, and never be afraid to say — *NO*!

Quick quiz: What's two of the worst things that can happen to an athlete financially? Answer — divorce and business deals gone bad!

Matters of the Heart

Athletes must choose the women of their dreams wisely. Most don't consider the financial consequences of divorce until it's too late. Athletes should be concerned about being involved in unjust lawsuits and/or divorce proceedings. There is a reported high divorce rate of 60%-80% for professional athletes. That's astounding!

In many divorce proceedings, athletes may lose half of their net worth. But timing is key. Some divorces occur in retirement, when an athlete's peak earnings period is long over and making a comparable salary to that of their playing days is virtually impossible. There is a tremendous lifestyle change when athletes retire from the game. This can also be brought on by *infidelity* — and you certainly don't want to risk playing that game!

Given the pressures of being a professional athlete, one should consider the benefits of a prenuptial agreement before tying the knot. It will greatly assist you in the event of a messy and ugly divorce.

If the woman of your dreams refuses to sign a prenuptial agreement, which protects not only you, but her as well — walk away from the relationship! It's not worth the headaches and daily drama you may encounter later. The same principle applies for female professional athletes whose fiancé refuses a prenup.

Professional Athlete = Instant Financial Target

When Business Deals Go Bad!

Have you ever lost money in a business deal?

You've heard the sad stories. I bet you know a teammate or another athlete who got ripped off by somebody. Or maybe the people you got financially involved with were legit and good people, but the deal just went sour. Either way, you undoubtedly felt the impact of it! This, unfortunately, happens more often than we think. Resist the temptation to make quick major financial or business decisions of any kind, which may increase your risk factor. Educate yourself and be open-minded to learn about the financial markets and the many products it has to offer. Do your due diligence regarding business propositions. Ask questions, and don't be afraid to say *NO*!

If something doesn't look right, feel right, sound right, or read right — then don't do the dang thing!

The Athlete Perception Theory (TAPT)™

I created this theory for my *Athlete Career Killer*™ book series. I'm introducing it here, but athletes will instantly recognize what it means.

It means avoiding the creation of, and the public perception of having an "entourage." This also deals with *peer pressure* within an "entourage." It's when you may feel like you have to "take care of" your friends from your childhood. You don't, and they should be able to take care of themselves. Realize that requests for handouts from family and friends will be plentiful once you turn pro. There's nothing wrong with helping a friend or family member in need, but not to the point where it becomes a financial burden to you.

If you're not diligently on top of your finances, maintaining an "entourage" can drain your bank accounts faster than you can smile and say *"unrestricted free agent!"*

Did you happen to notice the above acronym — TAPT? It was purposely created to sound similar to the word "tapped" — as in tapped out! That's exactly what you'll eventually become if you try to financially support an "entourage."

Certainly, it's all right to be generous to close family and friends every now and then. I'm not saying don't buy your dad and mom their dream house, because they surely deserve it. But don't buy your cousins and homeboys the same stuff you have and allow them to live off of you. At some point this will put substantial stress on you financially.

Some athletes depend on family members or friends to help them with their finances, and that could be a financially fatal mistake! Avoid hiring family members, friends, or the "friend of a close friend" scenario. It's just not worth the financial risk. Remember, financial professionals should be licensed and legal.

The point is, it's hard to say no to lending money to family and friends you're close to because, if you say yes, the requests will never stop. They may see that as a weakness in you, and keep asking for more dough.

If you're a rookie pro athlete, don't feel that now that you've made it to the "bigs" that you have to impress everyone — including your teammates. You don't have to live beyond your means to impress anyone by driving fancy and expensive cars or buying expensive homes. Just because you're now a "professional athlete" doesn't mean you should throw your money around irresponsibly.

If you're a veteran athlete who has been through a financial hardship and recovered nicely, become a *mentor* to your younger brethren, and pass along some of your wisdom and insights. They will thank you for it ten years from now, if not sooner. *I guarantee it!*

Keys to Holding onto Your Wealth

It has been well reported that:

- By the time they have been retired for two years, about 78% of former NFL players have gone bankrupt or are under financial distress because of joblessness, divorce, or from making poor business decisions.
- Within five years of retirement, an estimated 60% of former NBA players are broke, as reported by the NBA Player's Association in 2008.

The common reason for these shocking statistics is that many athletes who retire from the game still possess several cars, are still paying mortgages on two to three homes, paying massive amounts of child support each month and, in a lot of cases, are still taking care of family and friends, including their parents. This takes a major financial toll on them after retirement simply because the big paychecks they were receiving as professional athletes are no longer pouring in anymore.

Don't let this be you — the athlete holding this book!

Here's the first key: You want to maintain your wealth. You want to be savvy and accumulate *"generational wealth"* for you and your family for years to come by growing your estate to where your children's children, and their children, and their children — will be financially set for life.

Here's the second key: Once you have established a solid game plan for generational wealth, you want to live with what I call *"quiet wealth."* To me, this means quietly living a peaceful, happy, fulfilling, drama free lifestyle, without being "gaudy," and being charitable in the community – all in complete financial serenity.

Chapter 2

Choosing a Financial Planner

Skilled, highly qualified and honest financial planners and advisors aren't hard for athletes to find. The best way to find one is to ask your peers. Ask a seasoned veteran on your team, the coach, or even the team owner who their planner or advisor is. Seeking out personal references from others you know to be successful is just plain smart. Here's how to find the right financial planner for you.

It's not always easy for professional athletes to decide on the balanced mix of insurance, investments, tax, and estate planning. Generally, you want to seek a financial planner who will suggest broader-based investment recommendations based on extensive knowledge of your financial situation. After you have a few names of potential candidates, select three. Visit the office of each one and ask for a detailed statement of fees and services, a resumé and references. Then go back and make comparisons between them.

Make sure you go the extra mile to investigate the person before signing any financial agreements. Make sure they are licensed in their field, have authentic references, and can prove their success on paper, or lack thereof. Now, any company can *"cook the books,"* so be diligent in your search and research.

About Experience

Your financial planner should have, at the very minimum, three years of experience in:

- General principles of financial planning
- Insurance planning and risk management

- Employee benefits planning
- Investment planning
- Income tax planning
- Retirement planning
- Estate planning

About Credentials

Your current financial planner will likely have one of these following certifications or designations:

- CFP®, Certified Financial Planner

  The Certified Financial Planner designation is perhaps the most common designation awarded by Certified Financial Planner Board of Standards Inc. (CFP Board) to individuals who meet education, examination, experience and ethics requirements. It generally is regarded as the industry standard for the financial planning profession.

- AIFA®, Accredited Investment Fiduciary Analyst
  The AIFA is the first and only professional designation that focuses on the process of conducting fiduciary assessments. The designation is a symbol of ability and knowledge to advise clients of deficiencies in investment processes.
- BCE, Board Certified in Estate Planning
  The BCE designation demonstrates the advisor's expertise and commitment to helping individuals plan for the passing of a loved one and their effective transfer of wealth — chiefly how to maximize passing one's wealth onto a spouse and future generations while mitigating estate taxes.
- CAS, Certified Annuity Specialist
  The CAS designation demonstrates the advisor's expertise and commitment to helping individuals work toward their retirement goals with annuities as a suitable option. CAS is fully

accredited, and the oldest designation in the annuity industry. It is the only such designation recognized by dozens of Fortune 500 companies.

- CFA, Chartered Financial Analyst®

  The CFA charter, awarded by the CFA Institute, is regarded as the designation of professional excellence within the global investment community. The curriculum and examination process are intended to provide candidates with ethical standards of practice, and an in-depth understanding of investment analysis and portfolio management skills.

- CFDP, Certified Financial Divorce Practitioner

  The Certified Financial Divorce Practitioner designation is the undisputed professional credential for persons who typically assist either spouse of a divorcing couple to understand their options better and the decisions surrounding their financial scenarios.

- CFS, Certified Funds Specialist

  The CFS designation demonstrates the advisor's expertise and commitment to understanding mutual funds — to be able to evaluate and compare financial measurements and benchmarks of the funds when constructing a portfolio. CFS is fully accredited, and the oldest designation in the mutual fund industry — created in 1988.

- ChFC®, Chartered Financial Consultant®

  Awarded by The American College, the ChFC® prepares individuals to meet the advanced financial planning needs of individuals, professionals, and small-business owners. The curriculum offers in-depth coverage of key financial planning disciplines, including insurance, income taxation, retirement planning, investments, and estate planning.

- CTS, Certified Tax Specialist

  The CTS designation demonstrates the advisor's expertise and commitment to provide ways to reduce taxable income. There are a number of ways to decrease taxable income and reduce tax liability for clients.

- PPC, Professional Plan Consultant

  Administered by Financial Service Standards, LLC, the (PPC) designation is awarded to those who successfully complete the 401(k) Service Training Program™. This designation signifies a commitment to education and service excellence in the qualified plan industry.

- QFA, Qualified Financial Advisor

  The QFA designation is ideal for those professionals who may wish to attain the coveted CFP® designation, but may lack the bachelor's degree, experience requirements, or the time/money devoted to becoming fully CFP certified.

- RFC, Registered Financial Consultant

  The RFC designation is awarded by the International Association of Registered Financial Consultants (IARFC) to those financial advisors who can meet the high standards of education, experience and integrity required of all its members.

- RIS, Retirement Income Specialist

  Yes, all professional athletes will face retirement some day! The RIS designation demonstrates the advisor's expertise and commitment to helping individuals plan for a comfortable retirement — chiefly how to maximize income while mitigating risk and taxes.

- RPA, Retirement Plans Associate

  The RPA designation is earned by individuals in the group benefits arena who complete an extensive four-course curriculum and successfully pass the examination. The International Foundation is responsible for the overall administration of the program. The Wharton School oversees academic content and standards.

As always, conduct your own thorough due diligence. No one person or team of people, however well trained and skilled, know absolutely everything required to deal in depth with ALL the issues pertaining to a professional athlete's financial matters.

*List courtesy of Agent Broker Training Center.

About Fees and Commissions

Some planners work fee-based only, much like lawyers. Others work exclusively, or almost exclusively on commissions. Many may charge a combination of fees and commissions. It's your final choice, and yours alone to decide whether the quality of the planner's services are worth the cost. After all, *it's YOUR money!*

What to Ask a Financial Planner

Again, don't be afraid to *ask questions*. For example:

1. *What experience do you have?*

   Find out how long the planner has been in practice and the number and types of companies with which he or she has been associated. Ask the planner to briefly describe their work experience and how it relates to their current practice. Choose a financial planner who has a minimum of three years experience counseling individuals on their financial needs. If you're receiving investment advice, it's a good idea to work with someone who has been an advisor through at least one recession or down stock market.

2. *What are your qualifications?*

   The term "financial planner" is used by many financial professionals (and many nonprofessionals). Ask the planner what qualifies him or her to offer financial planning advice, and whether they hold a financial planning designation such as the Certified Financial Planner or Chartered Financial Analyst marks. Look for a planner who has proven experience in financial planning topics such as insurance, tax planning, investments, estate planning, or retirement planning.

3. *What services do you offer?*

The services a financial planner offers depend on a number of factors including credentials, licenses and areas of expertise. Financial planners cannot offer insurance or securities products such as mutual funds or stocks without the proper licenses, or give investment advice unless registered with state or federal authorities. *Beware!* Some planners offer financial planning advice on a range of topics but are not licensed and do not offer financial products. Others may provide advice only in specific areas such as estate planning or on tax matters.

4. *How much do you typically charge?*
   The amount you pay the planner will depend on your particular needs, but they should be able to provide you with an estimate of possible costs based on the work to be performed. It's vitally imperative that you ask the planner or advisor to provide you a written breakdown of all fees and commissions, how they are figured, and which ones are fixed and which ones are variable.

5. *What's your investing style? Cautious or aggressive?*
   Make sure the planner's viewpoint on investing is not too cautious or overly aggressive for you. They should offer you the right mix and balance of securities for your personal financial status. Some planners also require you to have a certain net worth before offering services.

6. *Will you be the only person working with me?*

   The financial planner may work with you individually, or have others in the office assist him or her. You may want to meet everyone who will be working with you. If the planner works with professionals outside his own practice (such as attorneys, insurance agents or tax specialists) to develop or carry out financial planning recommendations, get a list of their names and do your due diligence on their backgrounds.

7. *How will I pay for your services?*

   As part of your financial planning agreement, the financial planner should clearly tell you in writing how he or she will be paid for the services provided.

8. *Are you licensed by your state or FINRA in securities or insurance?*

   Make sure they're licensed, and ask to view it. Also, ask the planner to provide you with a description of their conflicts of interest in writing, if any. For example, financial planners who are employees of banks, insurance companies or investment firms often favor their own company products, even when they are less competitive. The planner may also have relationships or partnerships that should be disclosed to you, such as business he or she receives for referring you to an insurance agent, stockbroker, accountant or attorney for implementation of planning suggestions.

9. *Are you registered?*

   Not all planners are!

10. *Have you ever been publicly disciplined for any unlawful or unethical actions in your professional career?*

    Never be afraid to ask this important question! Your financial future as a current or former athlete depends on it! If the person squirms or seems offended by this question — run out the door! Several government and professional regulatory organizations, such as the Financial Industry Regulatory Authority (FINRA), your own state insurance and securities departments, and the CFP Board, keep records on the disciplinary history of financial planners and advisors.

Ask what organizations the planner is regulated by, and contact these groups to conduct your due diligence involving a background check. All financial planners who have registered as investment advisors with the Securities and Exchange Commission or state securities agencies, or who are associated with a company that is registered as an investment adviser, *MUST* be able to provide you with a disclosure form called Form ADV, or the state equivalent of that form.

Form ADV contains critical financial information about a registered investment advisor (RIA), and is kept on file with the Securities & Exchange Commission. Many financial planners do not hold securities or insurance licenses, so be persistent in finding the answers to your questions.

11. *Can I get that in writing?*

    Ask the planner to provide you with a written agreement that details the services that will be provided. Keep this document in your files for future reference.

12. *What is your opinion of my true financial situation?*

    Reexamine your investment goals, time horizon, risk tolerance, and financial circumstances. Have any of these objectives or circumstances changed? If so, will you still be able to meet your long-term financial goals? Allow your planner to assess your true financial situation by providing complete information on your current financial picture.

13. *What about risk in this economic environment?* Has your risk tolerance changed — or are you just feeling a natural unease following the downturn in the overall market and economy?

14. *Do I need to reconsider my time horizon?* How long is your time horizon? Are you a young professional athlete just starting out, or are you an established veteran? All things being equal, you can afford to be more aggressive if you have a longer time horizon.

15. *Does my investment strategy need readjusting?* If you're retiring from the game and withdrawing income from your investment portfolio for living expenses, talk to your financial planner about this next financial phase of your life — living comfortably as a retired or soon to be retired former professional athlete.

If you can answer "yes" to any of the following questions, ask your planner if you may need an adjustment to your investment mix to keep up to date with the following changes, as they apply to you.

- Did you get married or have a child?
- Has there been a divorce, or is your son or daughter getting nearer to needing money for college tuition and expenses?
- Do members of your family need temporary financial assistance?
- Are you now helping to financially support a parent or parents?

16. *What if I haven't invested enough for retirement from sports?*

    Talk to your financial planner about a number of possible strategies to help build up your assets prior to or during your retirement.

17. *Are there any new tax implications for 2010?*
Make sure your planner has a good game plan to legally minimize your taxes.

18. *What's your past performance?*
Timing of investments often determines performance. When a planner or advisor makes claims — which they sometimes do on their web sites or in brochures — you need to see objective evidence!

19. *What about customer service?*
Some planners and advisors may frown upon you calling them every time the market has a bad day or a bad week. Once you have an investment strategy in place, be patient, yet firmly persistent. You have a right to know how your money is being handled.

Also, ask what kinds of summary statements you will get? What if you call them out of the blue with a tax or risk question? How will it be handled? Make sure whatever arrangement you agree upon is comfortable with all concerned.

20. *What about your ethics?*

With tens of thousands of financial planners and advisors out there, you don't want one who takes your check intended for investment funds and "converts it to his or her own use," meaning embezzlement of your hard earned money! The NASD (National Association of Securities Dealers) publishes a monthly list of enforcement actions against brokers and advisors. Thankfully, most are honest and legit.

There's also the issue of whether the planner or advisor is a fiduciary. This means your interests legally come first.

Remember, *asking questions* is vital to your financial health and well being!

Chapter 3

Athlete Investment Options

Recruiting the Right Investment Broker

Remember when you were a high school athlete, and later, if you were fortunate, recruited to play college sports? *Let's flip that script!* I want you to now be the recruiter who's looking for the same "skills" that scouts and coaches sought in you — but from a financial standpoint.

A carefully selected broker can supply you with valuable investment information and make profitable investment suggestions. If you make the right choice, your broker can be your single most valuable source of help in making good investment decisions. By the same token, an inept or unresponsive broker can make your life miserable, as well as cost you money.

The first decision you need to make is whether you want a traditional broker, whether you'd rather do your stock research and trading for yourself, or get your advice elsewhere and use a brokerage firm only to execute your trades.

Brokers differ in several ways. There are full-service and discount firms, national, regional, and local firms, and firms that operate only online or over the phone. All sell more than stocks; they sell municipal bonds, unit trusts, tax shelters, and annuities, among other products. But the chief distinction is between full-service and the discount firms.

Full-Service Brokers

If you'd rather pay someone else for investment recommendations, then consider researching full-service.

Do you want investment advice and recommendations? If so, you're likely in the market for a full-service broker.

Mostly, these are the high profile national firms with armies of analysts who crank out buy and sell recommendations for a long list of stocks and bonds. Individual brokers assigned to your account will be called financial consultants or something similar. Rarely are they officially referred to as brokers. Brokers must be licensed.

Full-service firms offer a wide range of customer services, including research reports, individual advice, asset-management accounts, consolidated account statements, and seminars on retirement planning, tax shelters and other investment-related topics.

Where the full-service brokers separate themselves from the competition is in areas such as stock picking, asset allocation and breadth of research. The best way to start your search for the full-service broker that's right for you is to talk to people who invest. Who do they use? Why did they choose them? Who does the owner of your football, basketball, baseball, or hockey team use? Ask him or her! I guarantee they'll be happy to help you! They will respect you for coming forth with these questions because it shows you care, are responsible, and are mature enough to want to be an active participant in your own financial future and success, and as an athlete — so don't be shy!

Discount Brokers

If you're the self-serve type of athlete, with the time management, organizational ability, the desire to do extensive company research in considering an investment of your hard earned money, and have a successful history managing your portfolio, then this may be an option for you. If you feel comfortable making your own investment decisions and don't need or want a broker's advice, then there's no need to pay for such services.

Today, discount brokers offer a myriad of services like stock tickers, libraries of investment information, all-in-one accounts, and computer terminals for stopping by to check on the value of your holdings.

But, with discount brokers, you get execution of your order — no research, no hand holding, no advice! Most firms will make helpful literature available though, often including research reports from other sources, such as Standard & Poor's, Value Line, and Morningstar. Salespeople are paid a salary, not commissions. Most discounters also offer a long list of account services identical to those of the full-service brokers, so, again, do your due diligence.

Many discounters are also members of the New York Stock Exchange, with offices in several cities around the country. They have toll-free telephone numbers for distant clients, and most offer online trading. Discounts for trading stocks, depending on the size of the transaction, can amount to as much as 80% of what you'd pay a full-service broker, although 20% to 30% is more common.

Before you sign on, find out whether there is a minimum charge for trading transactions. Some firms set a $20.00 to $45.00 minimum fee, regardless of the size of the trade. On small trades that could wipe out the savings you might have anticipated.

Investments offer a dangerous draw — enormous rewards with the possibility of awful, financially crippling losses. Athletes love the idea of amassing wealth; however, no one likes to lose their money. The key here is to learn how to invest your money with minimal risks. It's impossible to predict the daily fluctuations of the market.

Never invest any money in securities you cannot afford to lose! Never invest without sound reasoning. Catching a market high is incredibly rewarding, but market lows are also part of the journey. *Don't make reckless choices.* Smart athletes make their money work harder for them by investing wisely.

Here are eight general tips to investment planning for athletes.

1. Identify and set your financial goals.
2. Understand the different types of investment vehicles.
3. Develop a strategy.
4. Implement your strategy.
5. Monitor the performance of your investment portfolio.
6. Review your investment portfolio.
7. Know that even the best laid plans could still fail.
8. Minimize risk, and don't be afraid to quickly cut your losses before they snowball.

Chapter 4

Credit and Debt

How much debt is too much? It depends on how easily you can repay the money and what you borrowed it for in the first place.

Warning Signs of Too Much Debt!

You're headed for trouble if you pick up these distress signals:

- You find it more and more difficult each month to make ends meet.
- It's taking extraordinary effort to pay your ordinary expenses.

- You've picked up the habit of paying only the minimum due on your credit card bills each month, and sometimes you juggle payments, stalling one company to pay another.
- You can't save even small amounts, and don't have enough set aside to get you through a financial setback.

Even if you seem to be getting along fine, you should examine your debt situation occasionally.

Pay attention not only to how much you have to pay each month for credit cards and other debt, but also to how many months into the future you'll be stuck with those payments. If you quit using your credit cards today, for example, how long would it take to pay off your non-mortgage debts? Six months? A year? Longer? Find this out right now.

Set a debt limit that considers what you can afford today and, just as important, what today's obligations are borrowing from tomorrow. If you're an athlete and debt is a problem, solving it should go to the top of your list of financial priorities!

Carrying huge amounts of debt is definitely the equivalent of a ticking time bomb, and is certainly a potential *Athlete Career Killer.* ™

How to Get Out of Debt

There are several steps you can take to ensure your credit rating isn't ruined.

Whatever the elusive "proper" level of debt may be, a lot of athletes are exceeding it. Despite generally widespread prosperity in professional sports, athletes have been going broke in record numbers, filing for personal bankruptcy like never before. If you see such drastic action looming in your future, it's better to take some steps now before your credit rating is ruined.

Consider rolling your debts into a lower rate loan. Perhaps you can reduce your monthly payments by combining your major debts into a longer term loan at a lower interest rate. This can be an especially rewarding strategy for credit card debt, which hammers you with the highest interest around.

As always, seek the advice and guidance of a licensed certified financial or debt counseling professional.

The good news is, if you've paid off your balance on time every month, you probably have a good credit score. And when a professional athlete has good credit, he has more choices.

Switch to a lower rate credit card. Credit card offers are everywhere, and card issuers will gladly arrange for you to roll balances on existing cards into a new account with them, provided your credit rating is still good. Just make sure you don't sign up for a low introductory rate that converts to a high rate after only a few months!

Check your credit record periodically. You can get a *free copy of your credit report* from each of the bureaus every 12 months at AnnualCreditReport.com. You can also get a free credit report if you've been denied credit in the past 60 days. Also, federal law requires the credit reporting firms to provide free reports to people who believe that their credit record is inaccurate because of fraud.

As of this writing, the three major credit-reporting agencies are Equifax; www.econsumer.equifax.com, Experian; www.experian.com, and Trans Union; www.transunion.com.

Come Clean!

If you know things are going to get worse before they get better, call your creditors and spill the beans. Tell them you that can't pay on time but are determined to pay them back, and you want to set up a payment plan. Could they possibly stretch out the payments for you? Some will. Some will even waive interest and late fees for a period of time to keep charges and fees from skyrocketing. If you get such an agreement, follow up with a letter to the company describing the terms you discussed. This protects you later if the company decides to change its mind.

Get Help!

If things are looking bleak and you can't handle it alone, consider signing up for National Foundation for Credit Counseling, which operates more than 2,000 local offices. There, counselors can help you set up a repayment program and negotiate with your creditors for reduced monthly payments and lower, or even waived finance charges. They can then assist you in setting up a more reasonable budget that allows you to make one monthly payment to the service, which then parcels it out to your creditors. There may be a small fee involved.

Save or Pay Down Debt?

Should athletes be putting money into savings or investments at the same time you're paying off a loan?

The best answer lies in separating good debt from bad debt. It's almost always a good idea to get rid of credit card and other high interest loans before you start setting aside cash.

Tips to Knock Down Debt

1. Pay off the high-interest debt: If you have high-interest credit card debt, tackle that first. It doesn't make sense to start saving or investing until you've paid off this debt.
2. Identify the good debt: For the most part, it's usually not a good idea to pay off your home mortgage unless you have a lot of extra cash. After all, Uncle Sam refunds part of your interest payment if you itemize your deductions on your tax return. Instead, use your money to invest in liquid assets. However, consider paying off your mortgage and any other debt you might have by the time you retire from the game. You can still live comfortably on less money when those sweet paychecks from playing are no longer coming in.
3. Save and Invest: Once you've eliminated high-interest debt, start saving as much as you can. One place to begin is your league 401(k). The next

best option may be an IRA. In addition to putting money into a retirement account, you need cash that's readily available in an emergency so you don't have to rely on credit cards. Consider setting aside enough money to tide you over for *twelve months* if your paycheck as a professional athlete suddenly stops, like if you make a poor choice and do something foolish and your league suspends you indefinitely — without pay!

Chapter 5

Estate Planning for Athletes

Surprisingly, some current and retired athletes *DO NOT* have a will!

Don't let this be you!

Live in peace — make a will!

Don't be foolish and ignore making a will, leaving your entire estate to be decided upon and divided by the courts. If you don't, when you die, your family will be left with legal battles for years to come.

For the record, just because you sit down with a licensed and competent estate planner doesn't mean you're going to die soon. It just means you've matured to the point where you're smarter about your money and more responsible than you ever have been in the past.

Steps to a Good Will

Writing a will is a sobering act that's easy to put off, which is probably why many athletes never get around to it. Consider for a moment what might happen if you don't leave clear instructions for the distribution of your property after you're gone.

If you die without a valid will, your state will supply one that is ready-made and devised by its legislature. Like a department store suit, it may fit — and it may not. The possibilities for trouble when you don't have a will are endless. A hostile relative might be able to acquire a share of your estate, for example, or a relative who is already well off financially might take legal precedence over a more deserving and more needy family member.

It makes sense to pay a competent and licensed attorney a reasonable fee to write a document that will lay out your wishes. Do some preliminary research about wills online to help you focus your thinking and get you ready to meet with your estate planning attorney.

Six Steps to Take When Crafting Your Will

1. Size up your estate. Start by drawing up a list of your assets — real estate, bank accounts, stocks, bonds, cars, boats, life insurance, profit-sharing and pension funds, business holdings, money owed to you, and the like.
2. Protect your children. If you have minor children, you'll have to decide who you want to take care of them if you and your spouse both die. This involves setting up a guardianship, a task that has two principle functions. The first is to provide for the proper care of the children until they reach the age of majority, which is generally 18 years old. The second is to manage the money and property you leave to the children and distribute it to them as you would wish.

If you're a divorced athlete, you might be inclined to choose a separate property guardian because the surviving parent typically would get custody of your children. Consider naming backup guardians in case your first choice dies, is incapacitated, or might want to relinquish the job after a few years.

3. Distribute your property. Next you'll have to decide how you want your estate distributed. This is obvious and straightforward in many instances, such as leaving everything to your spouse, or to your children if both of you die.

4. Choose an executor. Be prepared to name an executor (sometimes called an administrator), whose job it will be to see to the distribution of your estate and make sure any taxes, debts, and other obligations are paid.

Choose your executor carefully. Naturally, he or she should be someone you trust — a relative, a longtime and close friend, your lawyer, or anyone you feel is able to take on the responsible task of disposing of your estate. That person should be willing to do the job, so talk to them before you name someone who might later refuse, thus forcing the court to appoint someone you might not have chosen.

You also may have to choose someone who will step in as executor if for some reason your first choice can't do it.

5. Do your due diligence and ask your attorney lots of questions — because you will surely have many. Write them down if you need to. If your estate is substantial, as most are with professional athletes, consult an attorney who specializes in estate planning. Insurance policies, investments,

and home equity could make your estate larger than you think it is.

6. Change it if you want. If your situation changes in the future, you can always amend the will.

Changing Your Will Later

Life as a professional athlete is ever-changing, and so are your estate planning needs. After you've created your will and an estate plan, you'll most likely need to revisit them at key points in your life as your circumstances change.

Here are seven situations in which you'll want to re-evaluate your will.

1. You Get Married: Your new spouse doesn't automatically become your chief heir. Most states give a spouse one-third or one-half of an estate. If you don't have any children, your parents or siblings would get the rest. To leave all your property to your spouse, you'll need a will. You

cannot disinherit a spouse without her consent. If you are living with someone but are not married and you want your significant other to inherit any of your property, you definitely need a will.

2. You Become a Parent (or again): Obviously, the big question is how your children will be cared for if both you and your spouse die. Consider using trusts, perhaps in your will, to handle assets that would go to your children. Talk with your attorney to determine if executing a durable power of attorney naming your spouse or someone else to act for you in financial matters when you can't, would be in your best interest. Durable power remains effective even if you become mentally unable to handle your own affairs.

3. You Approach Retirement: If you've been blessed to play professional sports for long period of time, and are considering retirement from the game, your assets have probably grown substantially, so

tax planning could save your heirs thousands in federal estate taxes. As you know, in sports, injuries can happen at any time. If you're a younger athlete in the prime of your career and an injury forces you to retire, the same principle applies.

4. You Get Divorced: Review absolutely everything. The people in your life are changing. So must your estate plan. You need a new will altogether, because in most states a divorce automatically revokes the provisions of a will that apply to a former spouse. In some states a divorce revokes the entire will.

   Get with your licensed estate planning attorney to help you set up trusts to control the assets you plan to leave your children. And revise any living trusts to remove your former spouse as a beneficiary or trustee after a divorce. Do likewise with a durable power of attorney or a living will.

Also, unless restricted by a divorce decree, change the beneficiaries on your life insurance, pensions, and IRA.

5. You Remarry: You and your new spouse may have to plan for families from prior marriages, and for children you have together. Consider a *prenuptial agreement*, should you want to keep assets separate and nullify your inheritance rights to each other's estates. More about prenups later.

   You'll want to provide for your new spouse and still be certain your children, if any, are taken care of. To do this, your attorney may talk to you about a Qualified Terminable Interest Property trust — QTIP, for short. This trust can be set up in a will to give your spouse the income from the trust property and some rights to principal. But when she dies, the assets go to beneficiaries you have chosen, like your children.

6. Your Career Has Ended and You Move to Another State: If you retire from the game and move to another state, or any time you move to a new state, for that matter (active athletes, too), have your estate planning documents reviewed in light of that particular state's laws and your current needs.

7. Your Spouse Dies: This loss can leave you emotionally vulnerable to financial mistakes. Avoid selling your house or making other drastic changes for at least several months. Seek expert advice from your attorney. There may be tax benefits to disclaiming some of your inheritance in favor of alternate beneficiaries, such as your children, if your spouse's estate is subject to the federal estate tax and you have enough assets of your own, including liquid assets.

   You should consider getting a new will and, if needed, a revocable living trust. Execute a new durable power of attorney and a living will (which expresses your wishes in case of an illness that leaves you permanently incapacitated). Put these in a safe place, and tell people who need to know and who you trust, where they are.

Tax Planning

As your life and athletic career changes, so do the set of tax rules that affect you. The Internal Revenue Code now reaches into nearly every nook and cranny of athletes' lives, from beginning to retirement. The tax bill athletes owe each spring is based on the saving, investing, spending, business and other personal decisions you make during the year.

That's why athletes must be aware of their opportunities to embrace, and pitfalls to avoid as your life as a taxpayer evolves. The fact that federal income taxes are among most families' biggest annual expenditures trumpets the importance of tax planning for athletes. Talk to a competent, skilled and licensed tax attorney.

Steps to Hiring a Tax Pro

Professional athlete tax returns can be complicated. Athletes should hire a year round, highly skilled and certified tax professional for tax planning, like a certified public accountant (CPA), or a certified public accountant/personal financial specialist (CPA/PFS).

Picking the appropriate type of tax planner is the easy part. Actually finding the right person to do the job can be tough. If you're thinking about enlisting the help of a professional tax planner for the first time, or are searching for someone new because you're not satisfied with the service you're getting from someone else, follow these steps.

1. Get a referral: Ask your friends, family, teammates, coaches, team executive personnel, and your league, whether they can recommend a

certified tax professional. Then narrow your list of recommended tax professionals down to two or three candidates, who you will then visit for an interview.

2. Interviewing candidates: Interview them in person. If they aren't willing to give you a few minutes on the phone — or they want to charge you for the initial interview — look elsewhere. You want somebody who is willing to listen to you, hear what you're saying, and answer your questions in plain terms that you can clearly understand.

What to Ask

1. *How long have you been in practice?* You want someone who has been preparing returns long enough (i.e. several years) to anticipate problems or IRS challenges.
2. *What are your credentials?* Anyone can hang out a sign claiming to be a tax preparer, because there

are no licensing requirements. Look for an enrolled agent, accredited tax adviser (ATA), accredited tax preparer (ATP), certified public accountant (CPA) or CPA/PFS. Only a CPA can have the PFS, personal financial specialist designation. Check your state's licensing board and professional associations to assure that he or she is licensed, is a member in good standing, and has had no disciplinary action taken against him or her.

3. *Do you have any specialties?* This is important to ask if you have a specific need. For example, if you run a business in the off-season, you need someone who knows business accounting. Or, if you have rental property, look for someone who has experience handling this sort of tax situation.
4. *How much will you charge?* A tax preparer should be able to provide you with an estimate. Find out if he or she charges an hourly rate or flat fee, and whether that fee will cover everything or

will there be add-ons for planning meetings and calls throughout the year.

5. *Will you file my return in a timely manner?* And will you have time to meet with me throughout the year?

6. *Will you represent me before the IRS if a problem arises?* If the answer is no, run out the door! If you are ever audited, you want someone who will defend your return.

Chapter 6

Advice for Young Athletes

Are you a young athlete planning a trip down the aisle? Make a date to discuss your financial future with her first. If you're planning to say "I do" soon, save yourself some arguments later by talking about your money now.

More important than the cake, flowers, or even the invitations is preparing for your financial future together. Sit down with her, discuss your goals and expectations on a *mature* level, and come up with a plan for an effective merger of your financial lives. It may not sound romantic, but do it anyway! Quarreling over money is one of the biggest causes of marital discord and divorce.

Ten Questions to Ask Before Saying "I Do"

1. *Where would you like to be in five or ten years?* This question is the best way to start a money conversation. For example, does one of you want to go back to school, start your own business, or own a vacation home? And, if you plan to raise a family, how many children, and when? Discussing these important issues together will help you set priorities and identify savings goals.
2. *What are our assets and liabilities?* Before you can create an effective strategy to reach your goals, each person should fill out a net worth worksheet detailing his or her assets and liabilities. Once you know where you stand right now, it's much easier to move forward. Consult a licensed financial planner to help with your planning.

And if you haven't discussed it already, now may also be a good time to bring up a prenup. A prenuptial agreement spells out how assets will be distributed in the event of a divorce. Divorce happens. It's simply a common part of life in our society. With about one-third of first marriages and half of second marriages ending in divorce, it makes sense to protect your financial interests as a young professional athlete, or any professional athlete, for that matter.

3. *Should we keep our finances separate or combine them?* Some couples relish the unity and trust that joint accounts foster, while others prefer more freedom and autonomy by maintaining separate accounts. Or you can have both. Some couples set up a joint account for household expenses, while keeping separate accounts for personal spending. The key is to find a system that works for both of you.

4. *What about our investments?* Whether or not you choose to combine your investment accounts is, again, entirely up to you. Nevertheless, it's important to view your portfolios as a whole to make sure you aren't overlapping. If you both hold shares of the same stock, for example, you could be placing yourselves at risk should anything happen to the company. Check for overlap by making an appointment to sit down with your licensed financial planner.
5. *How will we handle daily spending decisions?* One of the first tasks newlyweds should tackle is creating a budget. Sit down together and discuss how much you expect to spend on groceries, clothes, vacations, eating out and other household expenses.

   The word *"budget"* doesn't have to be a bad word to be avoided for the young professional athlete. Think of it as a means to reaching your goals.

You should also take this time to discuss other spending issues, such as how much each of you can spend without consulting the other. You probably don't want to discuss every $50.00 purchase, but you don't want to come home from practice and *unexpectedly* find a new Rolls Royce in the driveway, either. For example, I just looked up the price online for a base *2009 Rolls Royce Phantom Coupe.* The asking price — $400,000. *Surprise!*

6. *Who will be responsible for paying the bills and preparing the taxes?* Discuss early about who'll be doing this. Have a game plan for success. No matter who ends up handling the bills in your marriage, make sure each partner knows where to find all the different account information, including web sites, passwords and bill due dates in case anything should happen and the other person needs to take over the responsibilities.

7. *What is your tolerance for financial risk?* One of the biggest culprits in marital money disputes is a mismatch of risk tolerance. You may be the type of young professional athlete who doesn't mind taking an investment risk here and there, figuring you're still early into your career. But your future spouse may be much more conservative and cautious than you are. Try to compromise on financial strategies that both of you can live with. If you still can't reach an amicable agreement, you might seek investment advice from a neutral third party, such as a licensed financial planner.
8. *What are our insurance options?* Adding a spouse to your health insurance may be cheaper than maintaining separate plans. Consider your specific health needs, then look at the costs and benefits of each person's plan. Combining your auto-insurance coverage may likely also save you money. You'll want to make sure you have enough homeowners or renter's insurance to

protect your combined possessions. And what about life insurance? Do you need it? If you already have a policy, either privately or through your league, do you need to change your beneficiary information?

9. *How does your credit report look at the time of marriage?* The good news is that simply marrying a person with bad credit won't drag down your stellar record. What's yours is yours and what's hers is hers. So, for example, if you apply for a car loan by yourself, your spouse's credit report shouldn't be a factor.

   However, when it comes to applying for joint financing, like buying a house together, lenders will consider both your credit and payment histories. It's better to know ahead of time of any potential problems than to receive the shocking news in the mortgage lender's office that you're stuck with a higher interest rate, don't qualify for as much money as you'd planned, or that you're being turned down for the loan entirely.

10. *How will we handle existing debt?* Make a pact to pay off your debts soon. Start with the balances that carry the highest interest rates. You may choose to work individually or collectively to pay off debts you accrued before the wedding, but don't add each other's names to your obligations. Also, consolidating your own student loans, if any, to lock in today's record-low rates is a good move — but, again, don't merge your loans with your spouse's. The commingled debt would be nearly impossible to untangle should you ever divorce, and if one of you were to default, the other would be left holding the bag.

Secrets to Marital and Money Bliss

Communication and compromise are critical to resolving money disputes with your spouse or significant other. But you also need practical money management techniques to better react to common marital issues.

One common conflict is — spending too much!

Sometimes a spender is in conflict with a saver, and sometimes two spenders stroll hand in hand to the brink of bankruptcy. In either case, each of you would benefit by writing down your goals — a new house, a Caribbean vacation? Make sure you're both in agreement and stay on track. Once you see where you stand in dollars and cents, one of you may be convinced that you need to spend less, or the other may feel more comfortable about spending more. (Hopefully both will agree to spend less!)

Chapter 7

20 More Money Tips for Athletes

Let's focus this chapter using pro hockey athletes as examples.

I also love hockey! I've been a huge fan since I was 12!

1. *Don't let your signing bonus change your life.* Athletes drafted in the first or second round to the NHL can receive a signing bonus in the range of several hundred thousand U.S. dollars, for example, but the majority of those athletes will not immediately go to the NHL.

2. *Manage your spending.* You'll only get paid for seven months out of the year. With a big check coming in every two weeks, it's tempting for young athletes to buy big ticket items and live an expensive lifestyle. But NHL athletes only get paid from October to April (excluding playoffs, bonuses and awards). Many draw on a line of credit to carry them through.
3. *You'll probably have to fund 50 years of retirement!* Most NHL athletes will play for less than 15 years, then retire in their late twenties or early thirties. Those who are injured will have even shorter careers. You have to start saving early and invest carefully to make your money last throughout your lifetime.
4. *Careful tax planning can make a huge difference.* For most people, taxes are their single largest expense. The multiple filing requirements of a professional cross-border athlete can make tax planning very complex. An athlete's country of

residence can dramatically impact the overall taxes he pays. Many Canadian resident athletes take advantage of significant tax savings by setting up a Retirement Compensation Arrangement (RCA).

5. *Fluctuations in foreign exchange can have a big effect on your finances.* Most athletes are paid in U.S. dollars. If you rent, buy or sell property in Canada or overseas, changes in the value of the Canadian dollar can have a big impact.
6. *Before you buy your dream house, evaluate the impact of where you own property.* In Canada, as of this writing, mortgage interest is only deductible if the property is used for investment purposes. For U.S. residents, interest on up to $1,000,000 (U.S.) of the mortgage on the main home or a second home can be tax-deductible. Consult your licensed tax professional for more specifics.

7. *Practice saying NO!* As a professional athlete, you will be asked to fund business and investment ideas, and make donations. Other people will ask you for money regularly, like family members and friends. Don't be afraid to tell anyone NO!
8. *Endorsement income can offer tax advantages.* Canadian resident athletes who receive endorsement income could consider setting up a Canadian corporation to take advantage of lower corporate tax rates. You will need professional advice for this advanced strategy.
9. *Protect your assets from lawsuits.* High-income and high-net-worth athletes are more likely to be subject to lawsuits. You should consider strategies to protect your wealth, such as setting up a domestic or foreign trust.
10. *Insurance and estate planning.* Consider protecting your family's future through insurance and estate planning. Ensure there is adequate disability insurance. Also, some forms of life

insurance can provide tax free investment growth. To ensure your family is provided for, it is important to make a will and plan to minimize U.S. estate tax, as well as probate tax. One common strategy is to set up a revocable living trust to hold U.S. real estate assets in order to avoid U.S. state probate tax. Seek professional advice.

11. *Follow where your spending takes you.* Often athletes will look at their accounts and wonder, where did it all go? Take stock and inventory of what you are spending and keep a running account for every dollar. This will allow you to see areas of your life that may be draining your wallet for no good reason at all.

12. *Learn to master the art of delaying gratification.* Wait before buying expensive items. Think about the money you have and how you want to spend it. Postpone making major expenditures until after your first completed year in professional hockey.

13. *Learn to live below your means.* Follow the example of smart wealth and spend less than you earn. Write a monthly household budget and stick to it. Devise a personal financial plan with your financial planner for your family that gives you opportunity to create true sustaining wealth.
14. *Look for opportunities to buy items on sale.* Wealthy athletes like buying items on sale too!
15. *Save at least 15% of your annual salary*, and don't touch it!
16. *Pay your taxes in full every year.* Except if you live in Florida, where there are no state taxes.
17. *Create an emergency fund.* Hopefully you'll never need it, but life happens sometimes.
18. *Have money automatically deducted.* Have funds from your paycheck directly deposited into a separate account only for your mortgage payment, or have your mortgage payment automatically deducted from that account by your mortgage lender.

19. *Review your insurance coverages.* Too many young athletes are talked into paying too much for life and disability insurance, whether it's by adding these coverages to car loans, buying whole-life insurance policies when term-life makes more sense, or buying life insurance when you have no dependents. It's important that you have enough insurance to protect your dependents and your income in the case of death or disability, so find out what's right for you.
20. *Keep good records.* If you don't keep good records, you're probably not claiming all your allowable income tax deductions and credits. Set up a system now, and use it all year. It's much easier than scrambling to find everything at tax time, only to miss items that might have saved you money.

For all athletes — if financial hardship ever comes your way at some point in your career, or afterward, know that if you remain positive, maintain a good attitude, and commit to continually educating yourself about the financial world we live in, you *CAN* carve opportunity from financial adversity.

Just keepin' it real.

Play Hard. Do Good. Be Money Savvy.™

PLAY HARD.™
DO GOOD.
CharacterAthletic.com™

About the Author

David L. Brown is founder of Athlete Safety Experts™ (ASE), Character Athletic Safety Academy™ (CASA), and University of Integrity.™

Personal Biography

Early Seventies – In junior high I received honors as a wrestler. I was voted an all-star while playing first base and right field on a team coached by my late dad. I also enjoyed playing my favorite sport — football — on a team with my brother. We lived in a beautiful little beach town in South Haven, Michigan.

During off seasons, to hone my skills in basketball, I attended Hoosier Basketball Camp at Lake James, Angola, Indiana, three years in a row in 1974, 1975, and 1976. Following the conclusion of the 1975 camp, I was honored to be named an all-star, and was the recipient of the "Pride" award, given to the player who exhibited the most effort and intensity during camp. That same year I was voted by the camp counselors to receive the Tom Saylor Award, which recognizes the player who demonstrates an excellent attitude and rapport with other campers, shows intense desire to improve himself, and is exemplary in sportsmanship and conduct. It was quite an honor.

The camps were great fun, and I got to meet, chat with, and get autographs from some of the all-time great players like Bob Lanier, Jerry Sloan, and Bob Love, and college coaches like Fred Schaus of Purdue, Johnny Orr of Michigan, and Tex Winter of Northwestern.

Late Seventies – After my sophomore year in high school, while I still lived in Michigan, my dad worked in a steel mill as a metallurgist and foreman. Shortly thereafter, a lot of plants in our area were beginning to close down permanently due to a bad economy. Unfortunately, Dad's plant succumbed to the poor economy and announced the plant would be closing its doors for good. It was tough on my dad and our family. We loved the area in South Haven, had made long friendships, and both my dad and mom were active in the community.

Dad, or "Pops," as we often called him, had to make some tough choices back then. It was, either keep his family in the area and find another job, or go where the jobs were. He ultimately accepted a pretty good job offer out of state in the New Castle, Pa. area. Our family later relocated to New Wilmington, Pa., a small, quiet town just up the road from New Castle, and home to the Westminster Titans and Westminster College, a private liberal arts college.

At Wilmington High School, I was active in football, basketball, and track & field. I was a 6'-3', 200 pound safety and wide receiver on the football team. After completing my two year stint in New Wilmington, I was honored to graduate as a two-time all tri-county defensive back, and in 1977 was also voted most valuable defensive back.

On the basketball team at Wilmington, I was a center, and considered a "rugged rebounder." I manned the middle, and successfully held my own against taller opponents due to smarts, strong fundamentals, and athletic ability. I played on a few all-star teams, and enjoyed the experiences. In track, I ran 100, 200, 440 meters, and the long jump.

In my senior high school year, I was recruited in football, my best and favorite sport, by the likes of Ohio State, Wisconsin, Louisville, Virginia Tech, and West Virginia University to name a few. My dad, family, and I loved traveling to the cities and touring the campuses. I was classified by college scouts and coaches as a "Blue Chip" athlete coming out of high school.

I was focused on football, track, and basketball, but I lost my focus in the classroom. I was a bright kid, I just didn't apply myself like I should have. Instead, I focused on sports and girls, like many seventeen year olds do.

So, in 1979, after the disappointment of not being able to play for a major college or university, I opted to sign to play football at a local school, Slippery Rock State College, which is now known as Slippery Rock

University, or The Rock, now in NCAA Division II. I majored in communications. The highlight of my brief football career at The Rock was the September 29, 1979 game at the famed Michigan Stadium in Ann Arbor, playing Shippensburg. We lost that game, but it was a great experience.

I later returned to college and earned an English degree from Penn State University.

Made in the USA
Monee, IL
04 November 2026

67386138R10059